# FLORAL ILLUSTRATIONS

## *A Treasury of Nineteenth-Century Cuts*

Compiled and Arranged by
### WILLIAM ROWE

Dover Publications, Inc., New York

# — PUBLISHER'S NOTE —

In a century far more attuned than ours to the natural world, botanical treatises, herbals, gardening books, and innumerable journals and newspapers poured forth a luxuriant bounty of floral engravings, continuing a great tradition stretching back to the Renaissance. In their decorativeness and extraordinary detail, these depictions both embodied their artists' styles and often revealed more than the photographs that would replace them.

The profusion of blossoms in this collection will recommend itself to artists and craftspeople in ways limited only by their own imaginations. And the sixty individual plates, designed as fanciful compositions by William Rowe, may even be painted in watercolor and framed to produce the most elegant pieces. Here, in some 750 original engravings, is the flowering world in all its beauty and singularity!

Copyright © 1990 by Dover Publications, Inc.
All rights reserved under Pan American and International Copyright Conventions.

Published in Canada by General Publishing Company, Ltd., 30 Lesmill Road, Don Mills, Toronto, Ontario.
Published in the United Kingdom by Constable and Company, Ltd.

*Floral Illustrations: A Treasury of Nineteenth-Century Cuts* is a new work, first published by Dover Publications, Inc., in 1990.

DOVER *Pictorial Archive* SERIES

This book belongs to the Dover Pictorial Archive Series. You may use the designs and illustrations for graphics and crafts applications, free and without special permission, provided that you include no more than four in the same publication or project. (For permission for additional use, please write to Dover Publications, Inc., 31 East 2nd Street, Mineola, N.Y. 11501.)

However, republication or reproduction of any illustration by any other graphic service whether it be in a book or in any other design resource is strictly prohibited.

Manufactured in the United States of America
Dover Publications, Inc., 31 East 2nd Street, Mineola, N.Y. 11501

*Library of Congress Cataloging-in-Publication Data*

Rowe, William, 1946–
    Floral illustrations : A treasury of nineteenth-century cuts / compiled and arranged by William Rowe.
        p.      cm. — (Dover pictorial archive series)
    1. Decoration and ornament—Plant forms. 2. Decoration and ornament—History—19th century. I. Title. II. Title: Floral illustrations: A treasury of 19th-century cuts. III. Series.
NK1560.R65    1990
745.4'441—dc20                                         89-23797
ISBN 0-486-26255-3                                        CIP

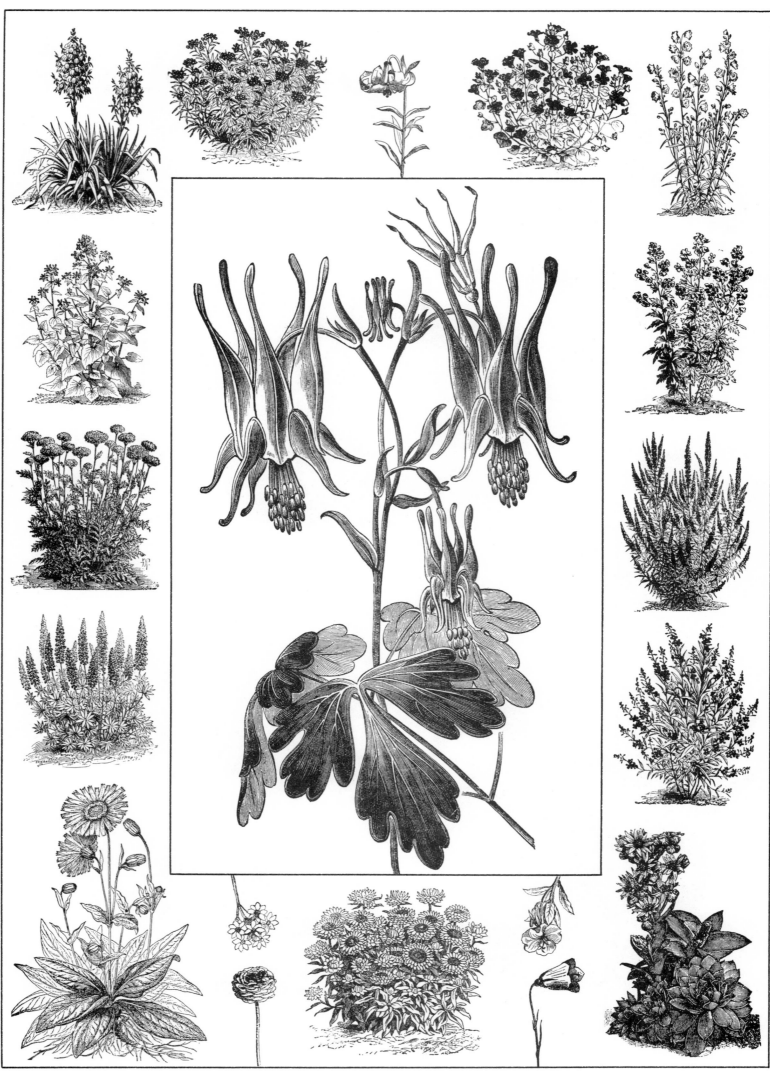

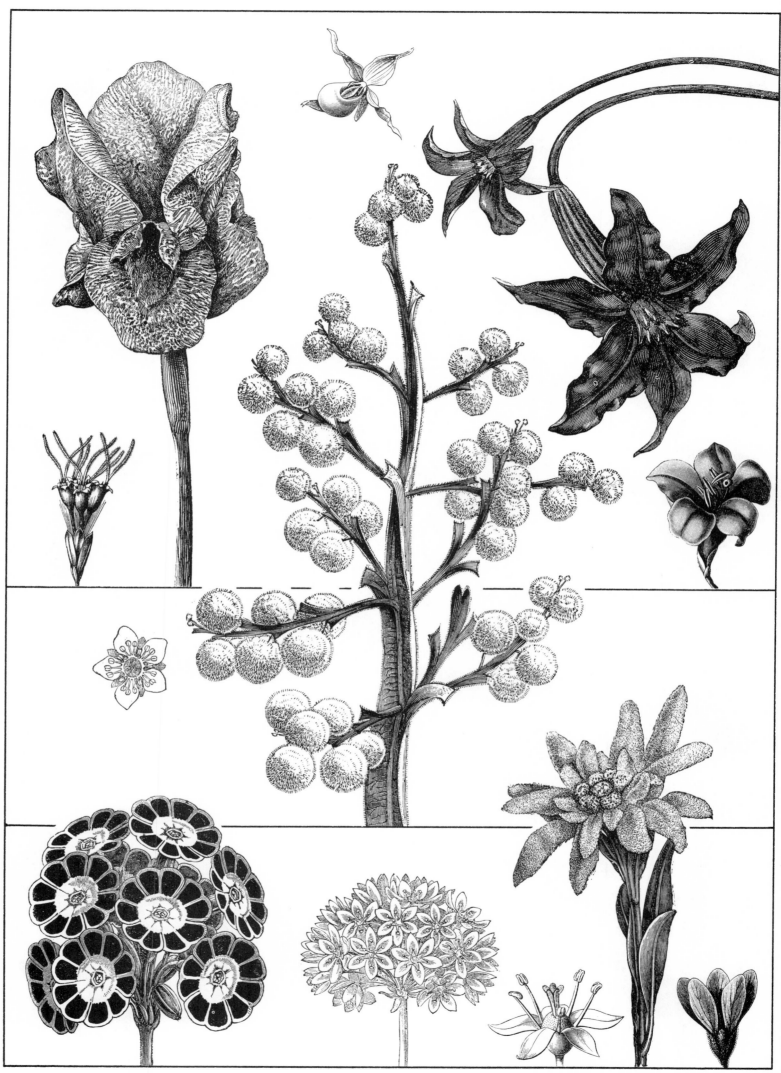

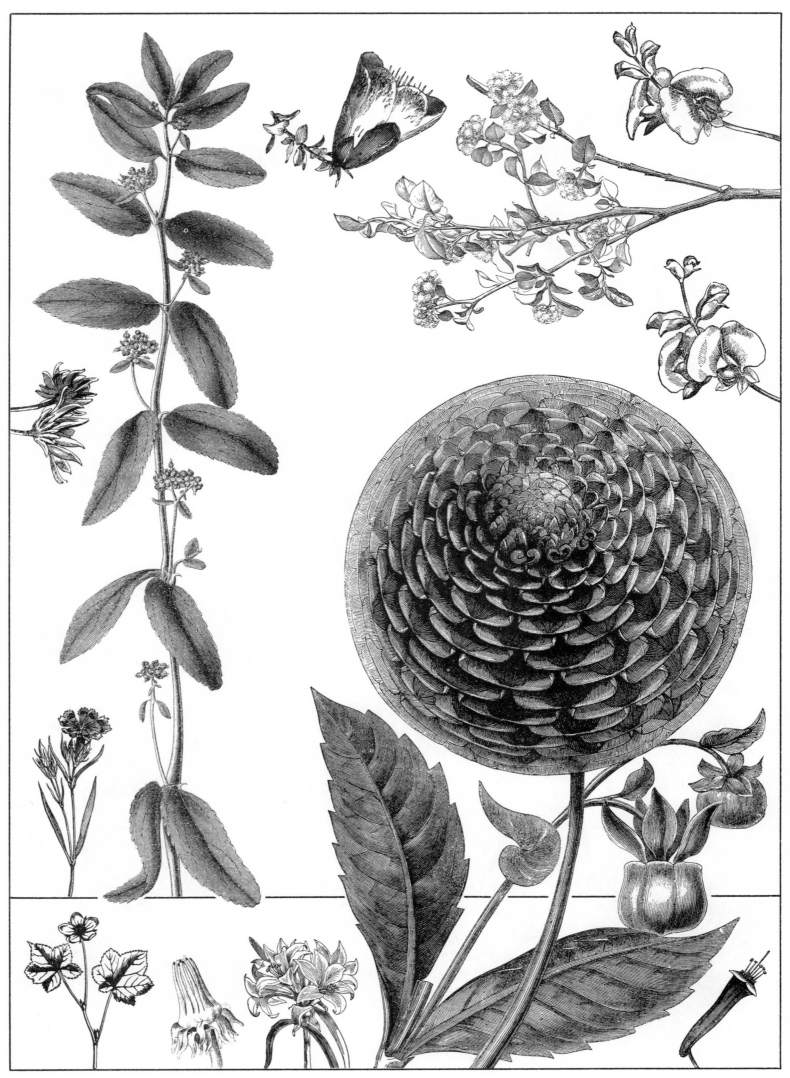

14

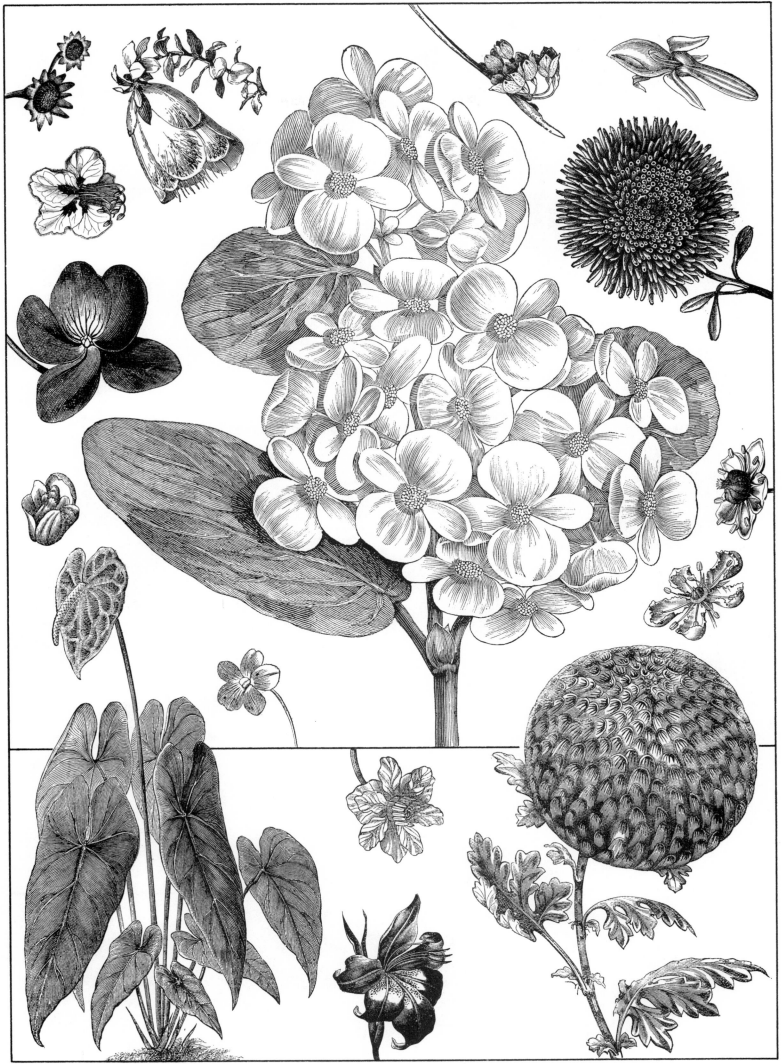

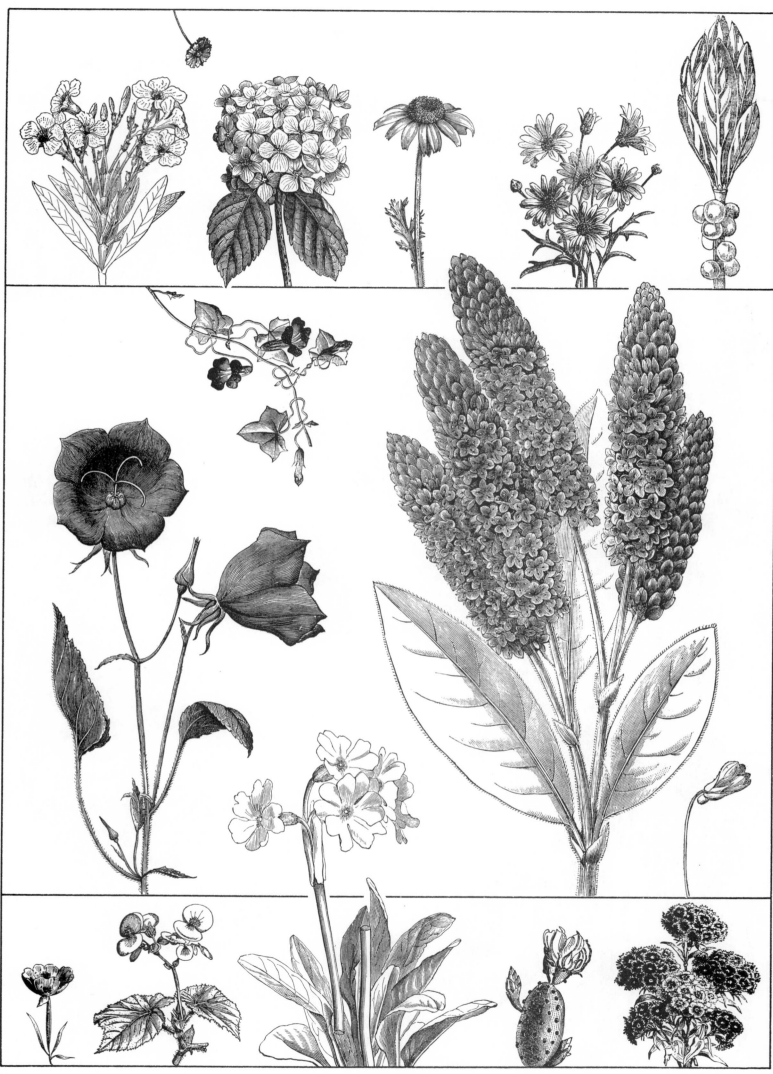

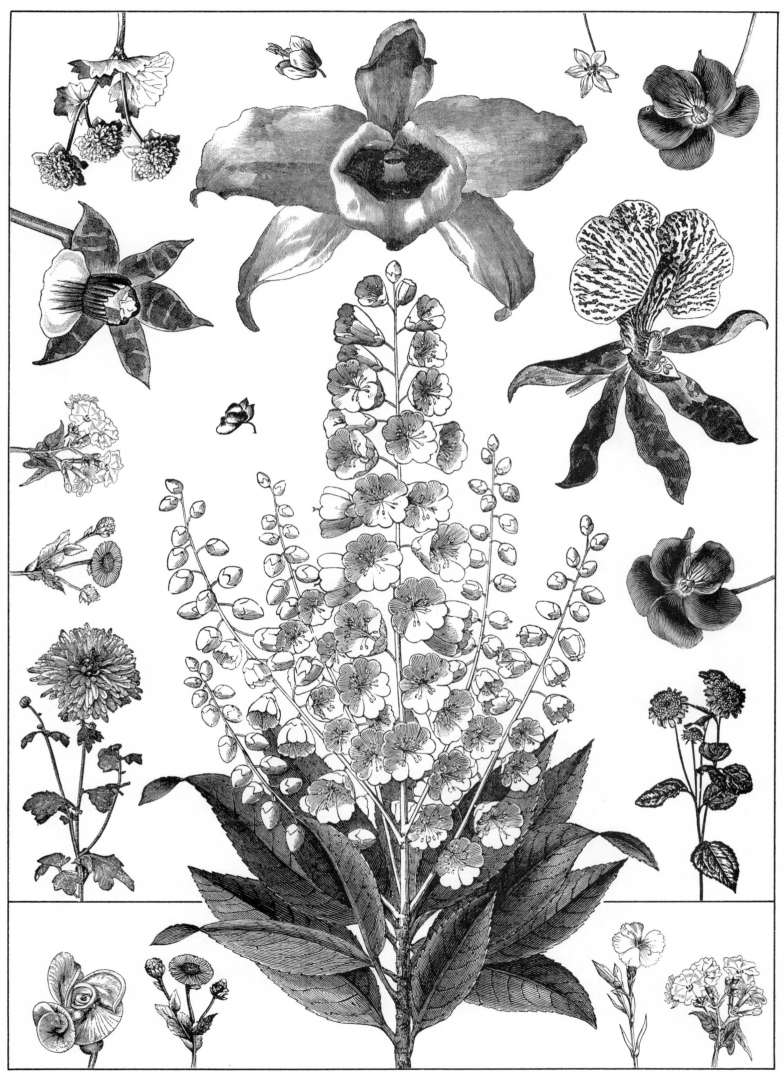

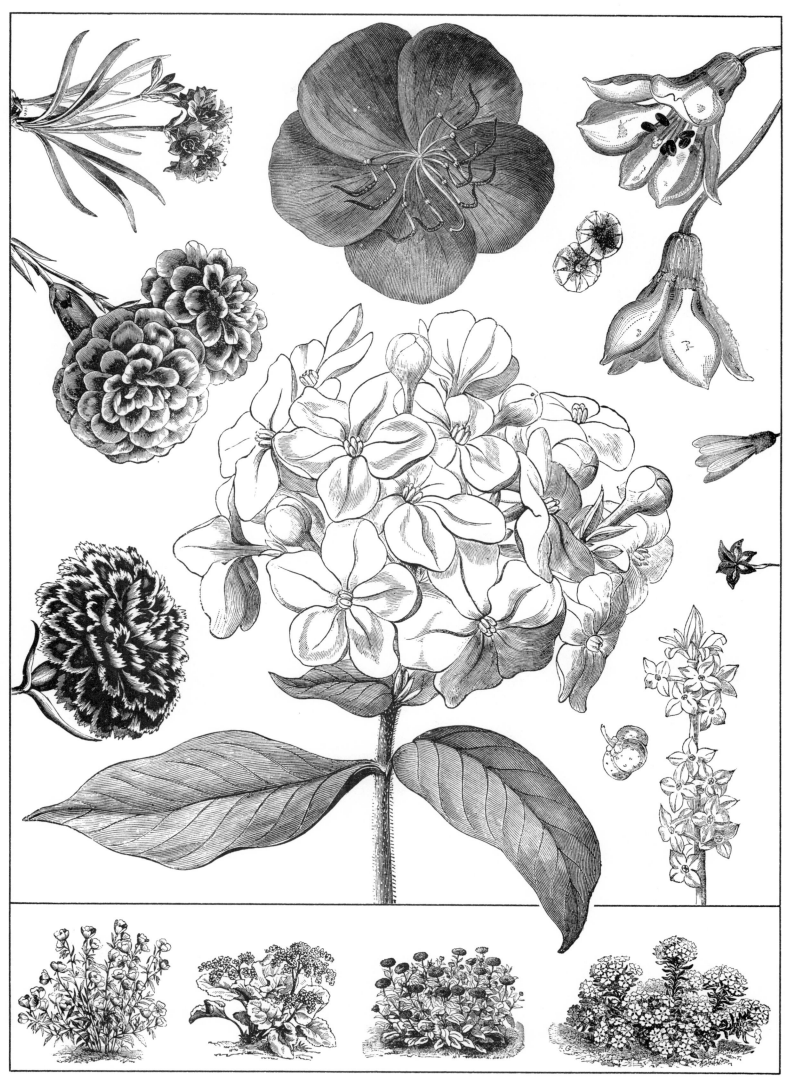

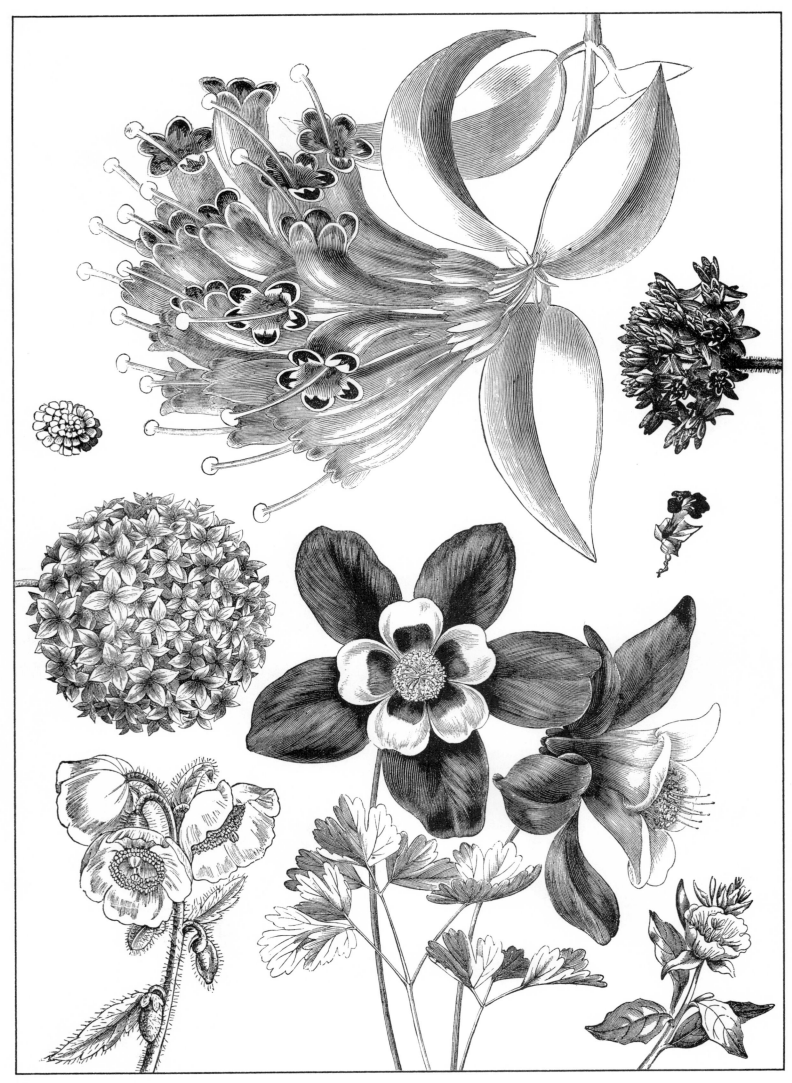

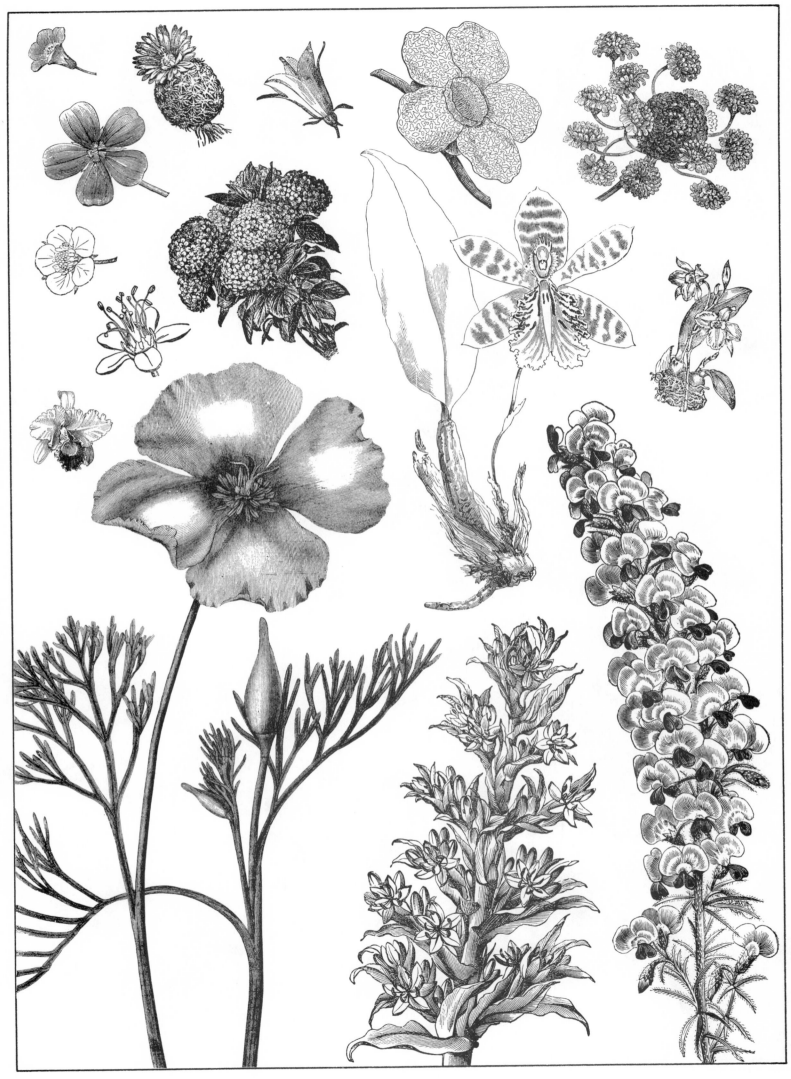

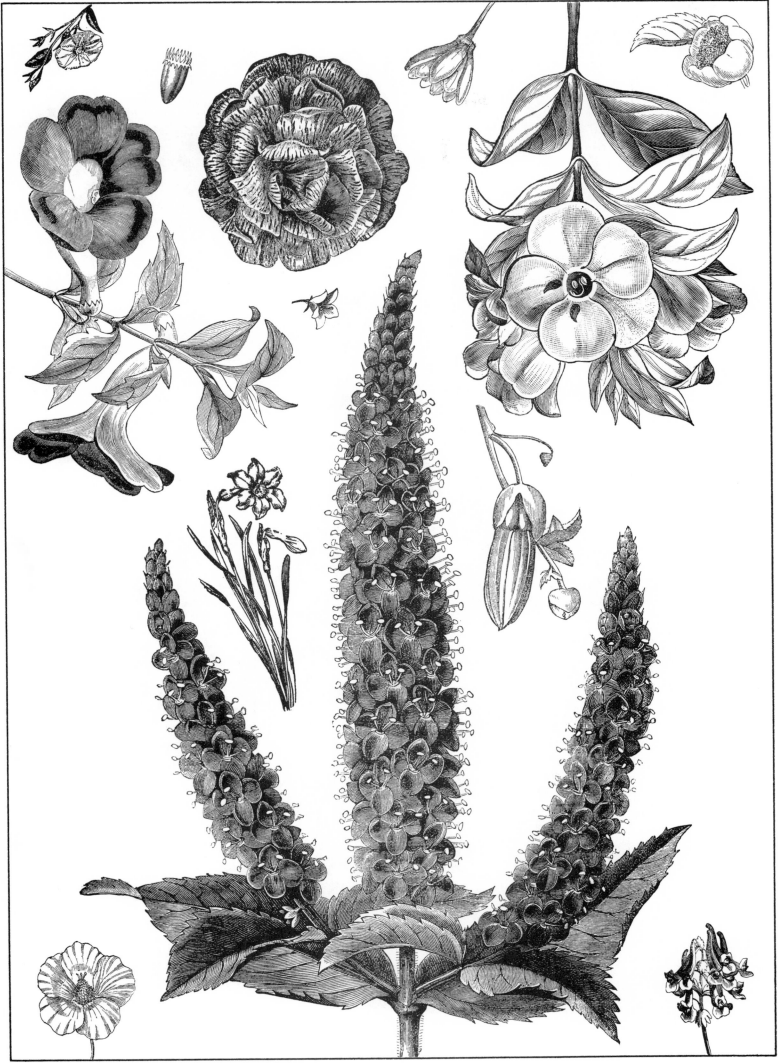

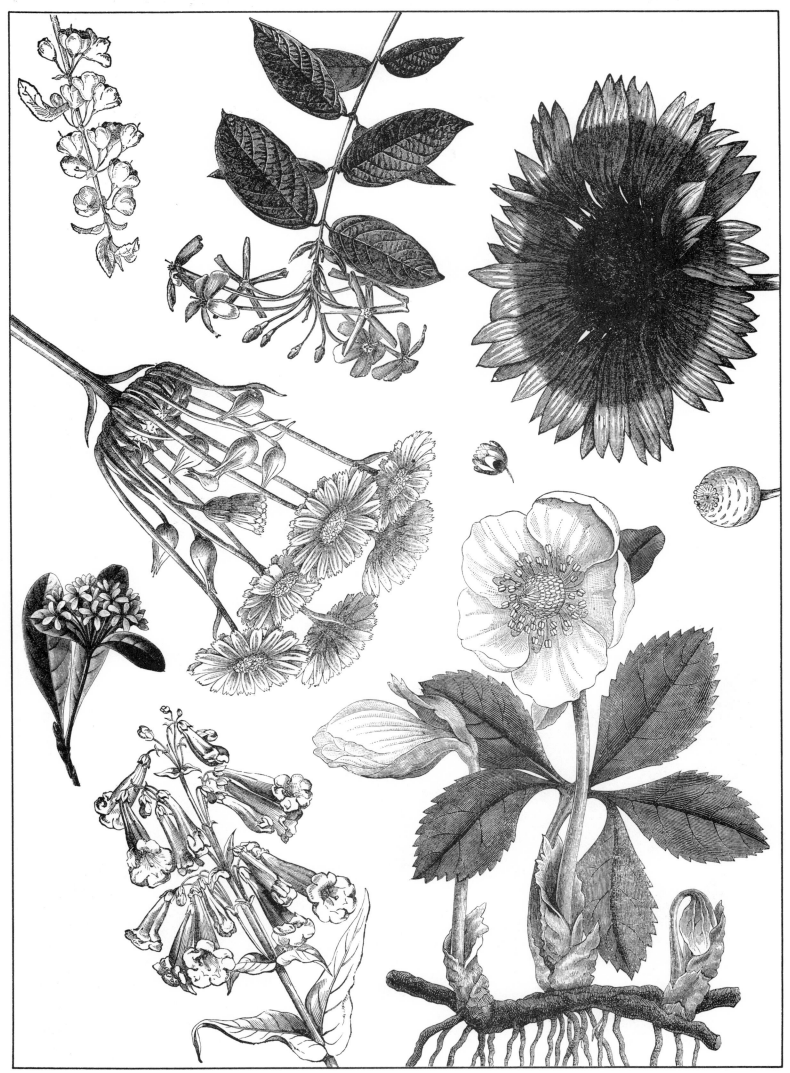

41

42

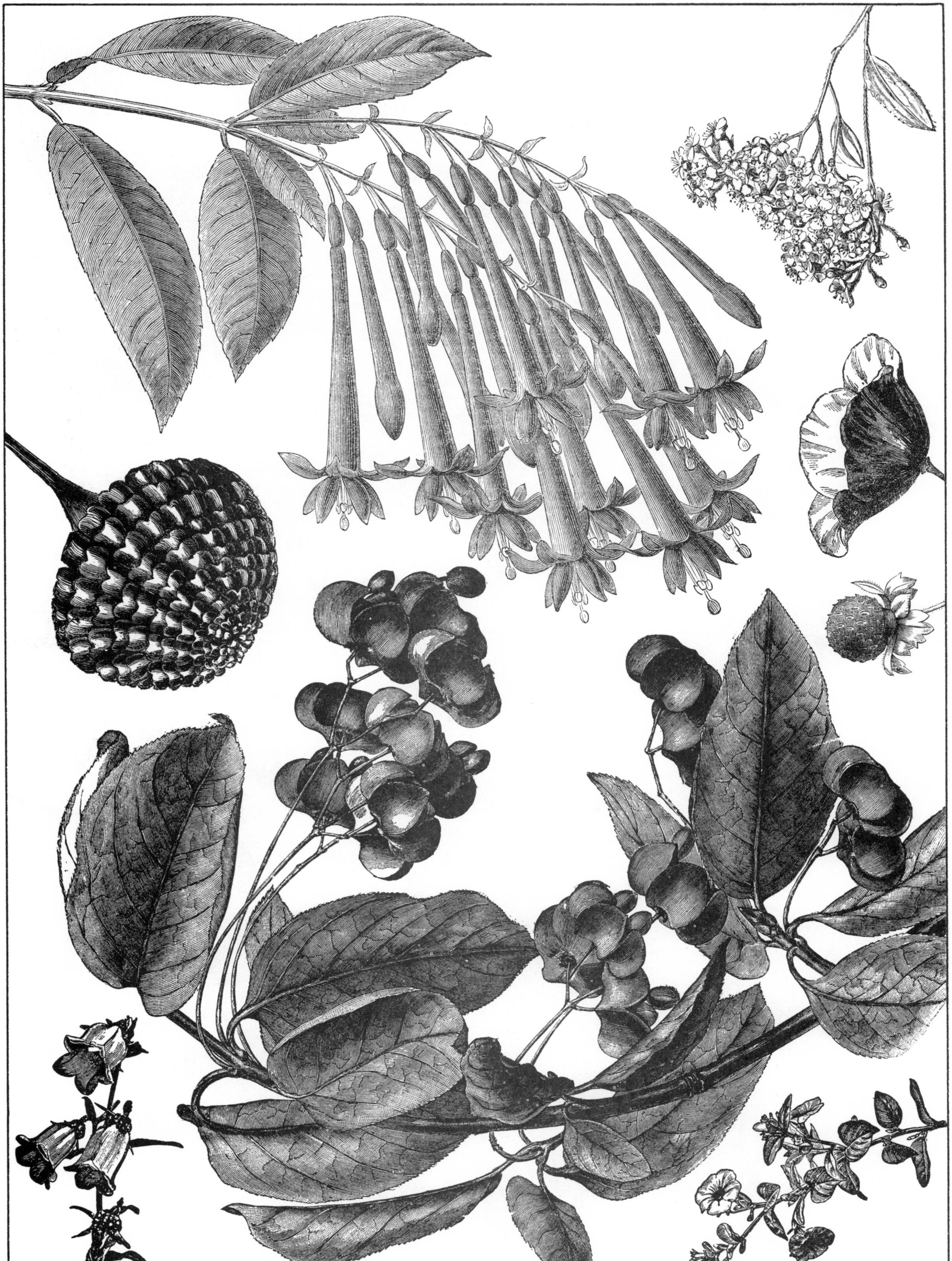

48

50

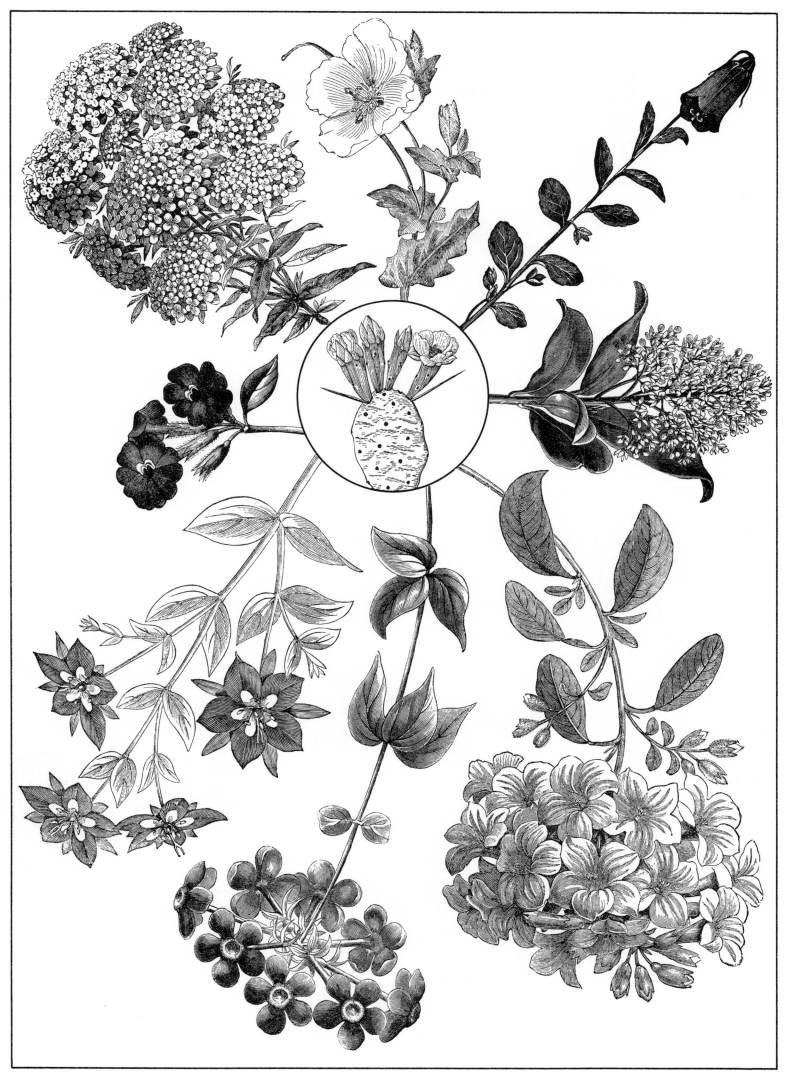

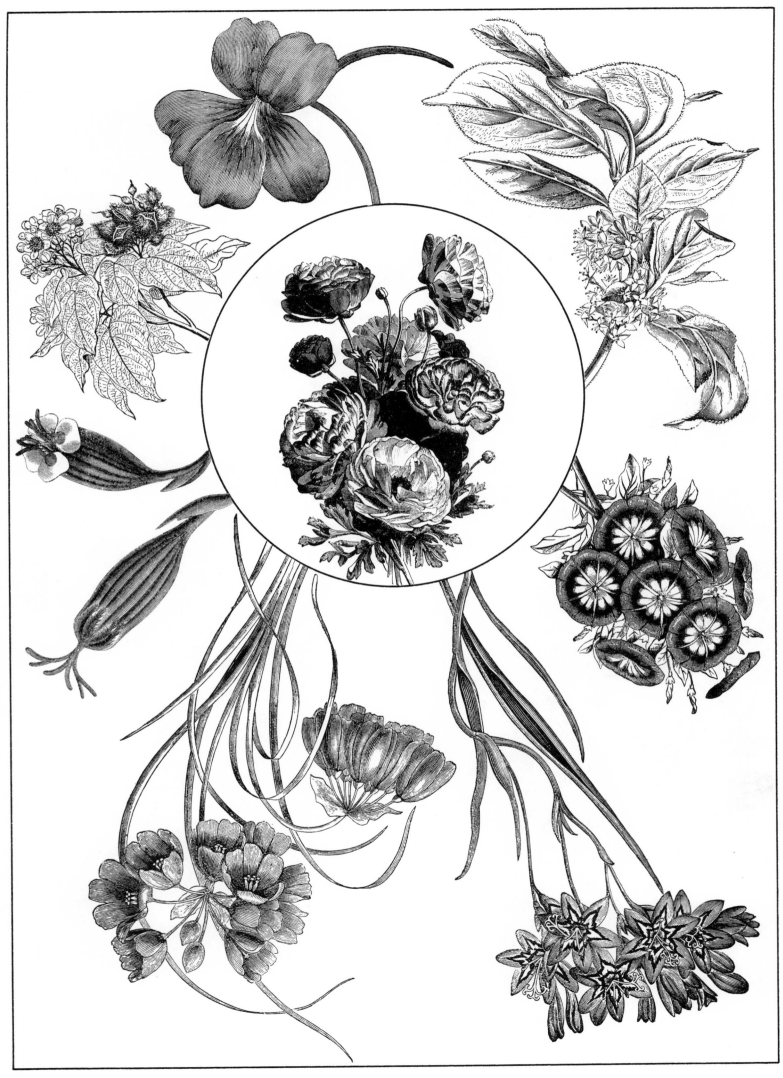

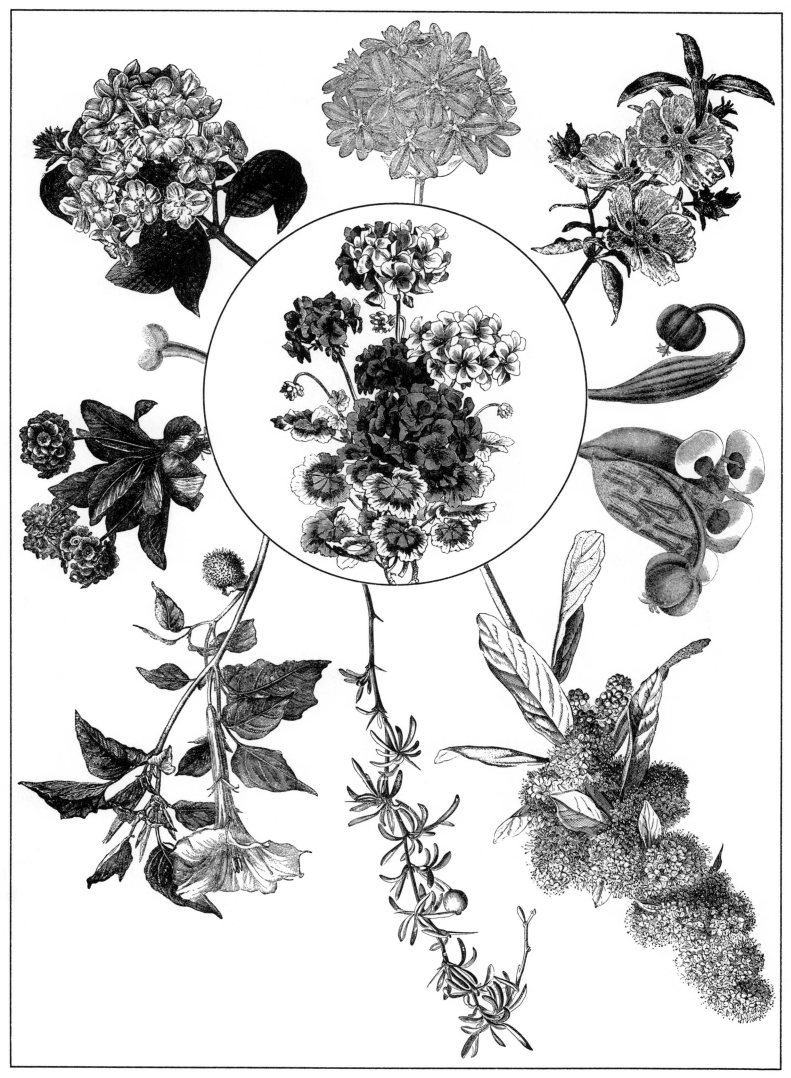